| | DATE DUE | | |
|---|---|---|---|
| MAY 1 4 2009 | | | |
| | | | |
| | | | |
| | | | |
| | | | |
| | | | |
| | | | |
| | | | |
| | | | |
| | | | |
| | | | |
| | | | |

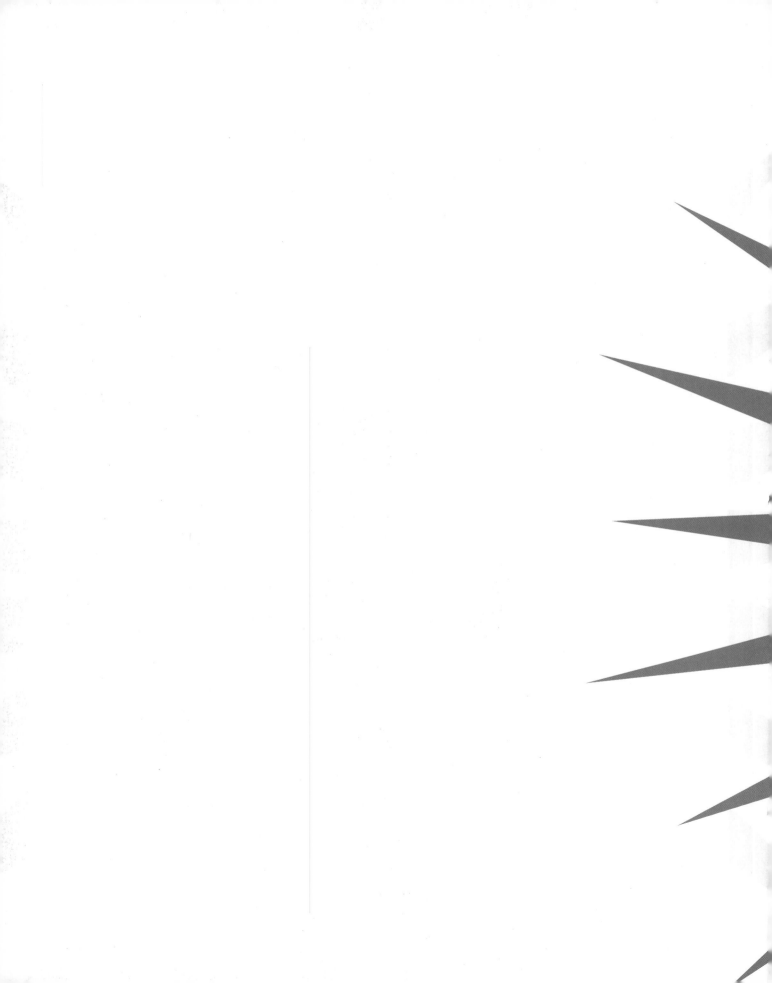

## How Your Body Works

# What Happens When You Are Born And Grow?

Jacqui Bailey

**PowerKiDS** press™

New York

Published in 2009 by The Rosen Publishing Group Inc.
29 East 21st Street, New York, NY 10010

First Edition

Senior Editor: Jennifer Schofield
Consultant: Dr Patricia Macnair
Designer: Phipps Design
Illustrator: Ian Thompson
Picture Researcher: Kathy Lockley
Proofreader: Susie Brooks

Library of Congress Cataloging-in-Publication Data

Bailey, Jacqui.
  What happens when you are born and grow? / Jacqui Bailey. — 1st ed.
    p. cm. — (How your body works)
  Includes index.
  ISBN 978-1-4042-4425-2 (library binding)
  ISBN 978-1-4358-2615-1 (paperback)
  ISBN 978-1-4358-2629-8 (6-pack)
  1.  Human growth—Juvenile literature. 2.  Childbirth—Juvenile literature.  I. Title.
  QP84.B27 2008
  612.6'5—dc22

                                        2007041765

Manufactured in China

Picture acknowledgements
Penny Boyd/Alamy Images: 15b; Clouds Hill Imaging Ltd/Corbis: 9; Education
Photos/Alamy Images: 23; Emely/zefa/Corbis: 11; Peter Gates/Alamy Images: 14;
Image State/Alamy Images: 20, 24; Sean Justice/Corbis: 17t; Don Mason/Corbis: 7;
Joe McDonald/Corbis: 6; Roy Morsch/Corbis: 18; Jim Munson: 15t; Photofusion
Picture Library/Alamy Images: 13, cover; Picture Partners/Alamy Images: 27b;
Protimedia International S.P.O./Alamy Images: 19; Wayland Archive: 17b, 22, 26,
27t; WoodyStock/Alamy Images: 21

# Contents

# Why do people have babies?

All living things make more of their own kind. Oak trees make acorns that grow into more oak trees. Ostriches lay eggs that hatch into more ostriches. Adult humans have babies that grow into more adult humans, who can have babies of their own.

Making more of your own kind is called reproduction. All living things grow older and eventually die. If they did not reproduce, they would slowly die out altogether, and one day there would be no living things left on Earth.

**Many birds build nests to help keep their eggs safe and warm until they hatch.**

Different types of living things reproduce in different ways. Lots of plants make seeds. If the seeds are in the right kind of soil and have enough water and sunlight, they grow into new plants. Many animals, such as birds, bees, and crocodiles, lay eggs. Often, the eggs must be kept warm and protected while the young grow inside them. When the young grow too big for the egg, they break out of it. This is called hatching.

Humans belong to a group of animals called mammals. Mice, whales, and elephants are also mammals. Most mammals grow their young inside their bodies until they are big enough to be born. After they are born, young mammals are fed on milk from their mothers for the first few weeks or months of their life.

**Human mothers keep their babies safe and warm inside them until they are born.**

# Grown-ups

Animals must be fully grown before they can reproduce. Most humans are able to reproduce by the time they are teenagers, but cats can have kittens by the time they are one year old.

# How are babies made?

Living things are made from tiny things called cells. Making a baby starts with just two cells, an egg cell and a sperm cell. When these two cells join, they form a completely new cell—the first cell of a new baby.

The egg cell is inside the mother. It is tiny—smaller than the period at the end of this sentence. The sperm cell comes from the father. It is so small it can be seen only through a microscope. The sperm cell has to push its way inside the egg cell before the two cells can join.

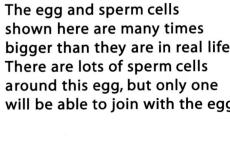

egg cell

sperm cell

The egg and sperm cells shown here are many times bigger than they are in real life. There are lots of sperm cells around this egg, but only one will be able to join with the egg.

As soon as the new cell is made, it starts to grow. When it is a certain size, it splits into two cells. These two cells grow and divide again. The cells keep growing and dividing until there are millions of cells.

The cells cling together to form a shape. At first it is a blob, smaller than the head of a pin. By eight weeks, it is as big as your thumb. The clump of cells are becoming a tiny baby. Can you imagine that you were once only that big?

# Doubling up

If two egg cells in the mother join with two separate sperm cells, they will grow into two separate babies. The babies are born at the same time and are called twins. Twins may look the same, or they may look very different. However, identical twins always look the same. Identical twins happen when one egg cell and one sperm cell join to form one cell. As this cell grows, it splits into two separate groups of cells to form identical babies.

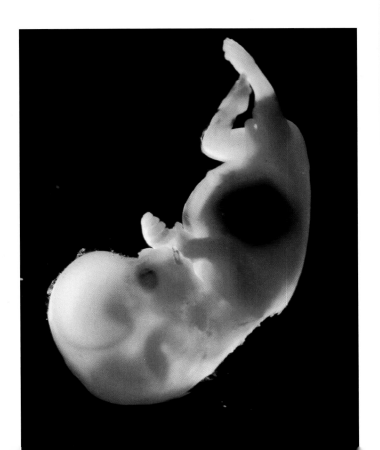

At eight weeks, the blob of cells has a head, arms, and legs, and is beginning to look like a baby.

9

# Life on the inside

A baby usually spends from 38 to 40 weeks growing inside its mother. The mother gives her baby everything it needs—warmth, protection, food, and oxygen from the air she breathes.

The baby lives in the mother's womb. The womb is deep down inside the mother's tummy, below her belly button. It is shaped like an upside-down pear and its walls are made of stretchy muscle. As the baby grows, the womb stretches to make room for it.

**This diagram shows the baby in the womb at about six months.**

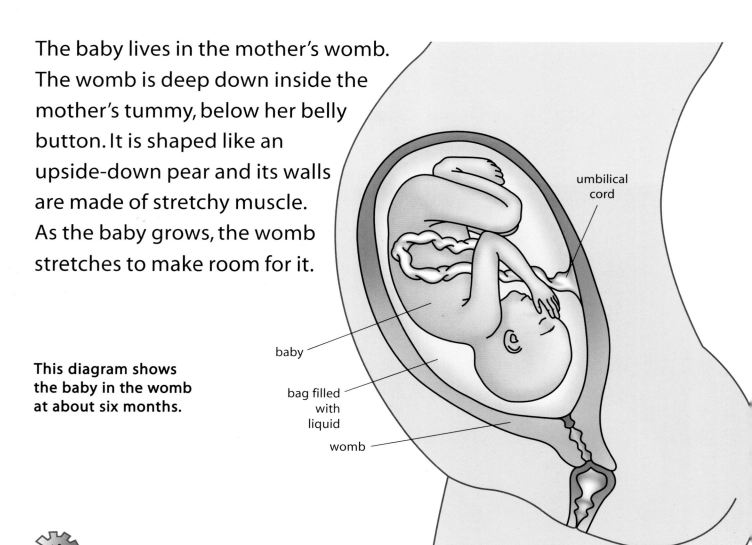

umbilical cord

baby

bag filled with liquid

womb

At five or six months, it is possible to feel the baby moving around inside the womb, and the baby can hear sounds, including people's voices.

The growing baby floats inside a bag filled with liquid. The liquid helps to protect the baby from any bumps or sudden movements. The baby and the bag are joined to the womb by a twisted tube, known as the umbilical cord. Tiny bits of dissolved food and oxygen from the mother pass along the cord and into the baby. The baby does not need to eat or breathe for itself.

As the baby grows, the mother's womb becomes bigger and bigger. It makes her tummy bulge outward like a big balloon. The baby moves around inside the womb, stretching and sometimes pushing or kicking against the sides.

# Passing it on

Everything the mother eats and drinks passes through the umbilical cord into the baby. Drinking alcohol or taking drugs can be harmful to the baby. If the mother smokes, the baby may not get all the oxygen it needs.

# Birth day

After about nine months, the baby has grown as much as it can inside its mother's womb and is ready to come into the outside world.

Before they are born, most babies turn upside down so they can come out head first. At the bottom of the womb is a small opening leading into a short, stretchy tube called the vagina. The other end of the vagina leads out of the mother's body.

**When the baby is ready to be born, it pushes against the opening to the womb.**

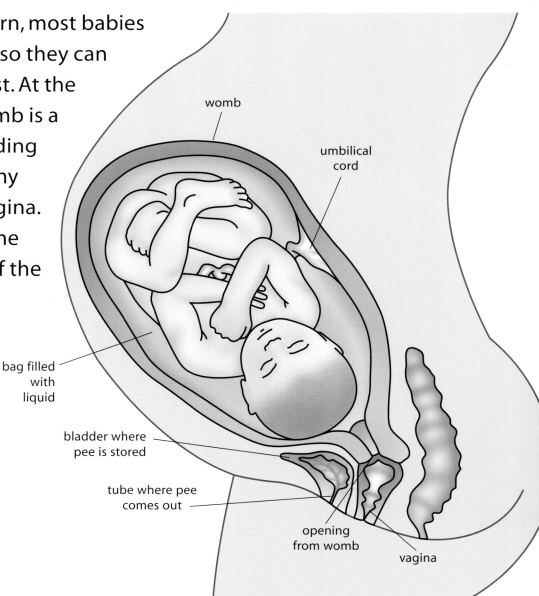

womb

umbilical cord

bag filled with liquid

bladder where pee is stored

tube where pee comes out

opening from womb

vagina

The birth starts when the walls of the mother's womb begin to squeeze and relax, slowly pushing the baby toward the opening. As the baby's head presses against the opening, it stretches wider. When the opening is about 4 inches (10 centimeters) across, the mother squeezes her stomach muscles hard to help push the baby's head into the vagina. The vagina stretches wide to let the baby through. Once the head is out, the rest of the baby's body quickly follows.

As soon as possible after the birth, the baby is held and cuddled by its mother.

As soon as the baby is born, it starts to breathe. The baby and mother are still linked by the umbilical cord, but now the cord can be cut since it is not needed any more. A short time after the baby is born, the empty bag and the rest of the umbilical cord are pushed out of the mother.

# See for yourself

## Buttoned up

Your belly button, or navel, is where your umbilical cord was. When the cord was cut, a short piece of it was left sticking out of your tummy. After a few days, it dried up and dropped off, leaving behind your belly button.

# The first year

Newborn babies cannot do anything for themselves, not even sit up. They have to be fed, kept warm and clean, and given a safe and quiet place to sleep.

For the first few months, babies are fed only on milk and clean water. Many babies suck milk from their mother's breasts. Breast milk is full of goodness and helps the baby to fight off germs. Babies can also be fed on formula milk—a milk powder mixed with water. The baby sucks formula milk from a bottle.

Babies cannot control when they pee or poo, so they have to wear diapers to soak everything up.

Young babies get tired quickly and sleep for much of the day and night. The outside world is a confusing place to a baby and there are lots of things to learn.

Babies cannot talk so the only way they can let you know if they are hungry, tired, or need anything is by crying. Newborn babies often cry a lot.

Babies learn really quickly. They watch the world around them and soon begin to pick up things and look at them. They start to copy the sounds they hear, and begin to eat other food as well as milk. By the end of their first year, they can sit up and crawl around, and may even be starting to walk and talk.

Babies love to be cuddled and talked to by other members of the family as well as their parents.

# A big baby

A baby elephant grows for almost two years inside its mother's womb. One hour after its birth, it can stand up and walk. But it still has a lot to learn—such as how to control its long, floppy trunk.

# Childhood

A one-year-old child is almost twice as big as when it was born, and over the next few years, it will double in size again.

Babies have large heads and short arms and legs. As a baby grows into a child, it does not just get bigger, its shape changes, too. Its arms, legs, and body grow longer so the size of its head looks less large.

By the time they are three years old, many children no longer wear diapers and can talk in simple sentences. Most have grown their first set of teeth. At about six-years old, children start to lose their baby teeth and grow adult teeth.

**A baby's head is very big compared to the rest of its body. This changes as the child gets older and the body, arms, and legs get longer.**

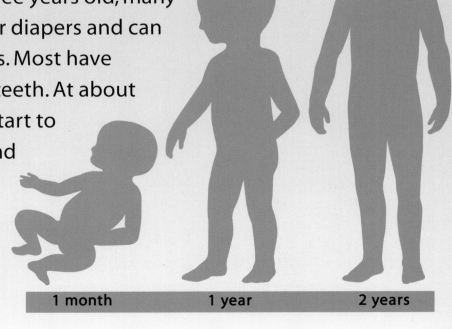

| 1 month | 1 year | 2 years |

As they get older, children are able to learn more difficult skills.

Children are learning all the time. By the time they are five or six, they can run and play games, and are already at school. In school, they learn to read, write, and do sums. They also learn how to get along with other children and adults. At ten years old, most children can feed, dress, and do many things for themselves, but they still need the care and protection of their family.

# New for old

Humans grow two sets of teeth in their lifetime. The first set falls out during childhood and is gradually replaced by adult teeth. The very last teeth to grow are at the back of the mouth. They are known as "wisdom teeth" and they do not arrive until we are at least 18 years old.

# Being a teenager

Between the ages of about 10 and 14, our bodies begin a whole new stage of growth. This is the time known as puberty, when we grow from a child into an adult.

Your body does not only get a lot taller during puberty, all kinds of other changes happen as well. These changes make your body ready to have babies of your own.

Girls often start puberty before boys, but boys go on growing for longer. By the time they are 18, many boys will be taller than girls of the same age.

Girls grow breasts and their hips get wider. Hair grows under their arms and between their legs. Girls are born with all their egg cells already inside them, but the eggs cannot make babies until puberty happens. After puberty, one egg cell travels through the womb each month, ready to meet a sperm cell. If the egg cell and sperm cell do not meet, the egg passes out through the vagina with a little blood each month as a period.

During puberty, boys' bodies change, too. The soft, wrinkly bag behind their penis, called the scrotum, gets bigger because this is where sperm cells are made. Boys start making sperm cells during puberty. Their penis, chest, and shoulders grow bigger, too. Hair grows under their arms, around their penis, and on their face, and their voice gets deeper.

# Changing times

So many changes happen to your body during puberty that they can sometimes make you feel confused or unhappy. If this happens, it is a good idea to talk about it with friends or family.

# Being an adult

By the time we are 20 years old, most of us will be as tall as we are ever going to be. We are now adults, and our bodies have stopped growing—but they do not stop changing.

Our bodies change throughout our life. Our shape may change if we get fatter or thinner. As we get older, we might lose some of the hair on our heads. Our skin will become less stretchy, and wrinkles will appear on our face and body. Our muscles may become stiffer, and our bones more brittle so they may break more easily.

**People go through lots of different stages in our lives, and each stage brings us new things to learn and do.**

As we grow older, some of the cells in our body wear out or do not work as well. Most men continue making sperm cells until they are at least 70. Most women stop releasing egg cells by the time they are about 55, and so cannot make babies any longer. As people get older, they are also more likely to get sick.

The length of time someone can expect to live varies from person to person and place to place. If people have enough food to eat, keep their brain and body active, and have medicines to help when they are sick, they can live for 90 years or more.

**People often find that when they get older they have more time to do things they really enjoy.**

## See for yourself

### Growing older

Ask your parents or grandparents if you can look at some photographs of them at different ages. Can you see how their faces and bodies have changed as they grew older? Can you recognize things about them that have not changed, such as the shape of their mouth?

# The same but different

We are all born the same way and go through the same kind of growing stages—but every one is also unique. This means that no one is exactly the same as anyone else in the world.

We do not all reach puberty at the same time, or grow to the same height or weight, even at the same age. We have different-colored eyes, hair, and skin. Some of us have curly hair and some have straight hair. Some of us have big feet and some have small feet.

**Families are all different, too. Children may be looked after by one parent or both, or by their grandparents. Some parents cannot take care of their own children, so the children live with other families.**

You were made from your mother's egg cell and your father's sperm cell, so you may look a little bit like one or even both of your parents. You might have the same hair color, for example, or the same shaped nose. But you might not look like your parents at all, and your brothers or sisters may not either.

Children often stay with their family for a long time, even after they are fully grown. Before we can leave home, we need to learn skills that will help us to work and take care of ourselves. Our brains are able to learn new things all though our lives, but the way that we learn and the skills we develop are also unique to each of us.

When we have finished school, many of us then learn additional skills that will help us to get a job.

## Animal families

Different animals care for their young in different ways. In a pride of lions, any lioness will give milk to a hungry cub, even if she is not its mother. Among ostriches, the males sit on the eggs until they hatch, rather than the females.

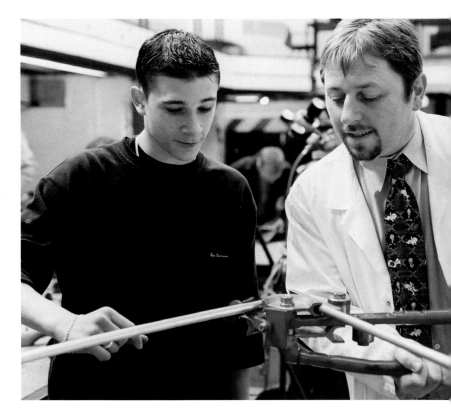

# Life cycles

The way an animal is born, lives, reproduces, and dies is called its life cycle. All animals die, but they are replaced with young animals of the same kind, and this keeps their life cycle going.

The human life cycle begins when an egg cell joins with a sperm cell and makes a baby. The baby is born, grows into a child, becomes an adult, then grows old and dies. Before this happens, though, many adults produce babies of their own, and many of these babies will also grow up to have children.

The number of humans that live in the world at any one time is called the population. There are 6.5 billion people in the world today and the number is still growing.

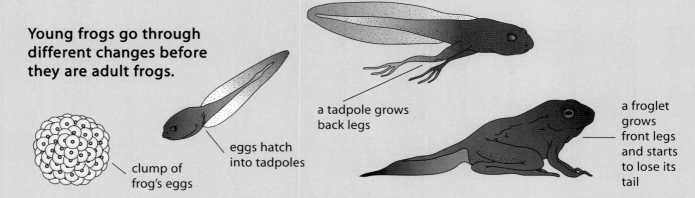

**Young frogs go through different changes before they are adult frogs.**

clump of frog's eggs

eggs hatch into tadpoles

a tadpole grows back legs

a froglet grows front legs and starts to lose its tail

adult frog

Other animals have different life cycles. Frogs can live on land but usually lay their eggs in water. A female frog may lay hundreds or even thousands of eggs, which all clump together. About a week later, the eggs hatch into tiny, wriggly tadpoles.

The tadpoles swim around and feed on water plants. After about eight weeks, each tadpole grows a pair of back legs, and then a pair of front legs. The tadpole is now a froglet. As the froglet gets bigger its tail slowly shrinks. Finally, the froglet's tail disappears and it becomes a frog. It can now start living on land, and make eggs and tadpoles of its own.

# Dying out

If a type of animal cannot reproduce enough of its own kind to replace those that die, it becomes extinct. This means that type of animal dies out and disappears from the Earth forever. Today, animals such as tigers are in danger of extinction, because too many of them are hunted and there are fewer places where they can live safely and reproduce.

# Looking after yourself

You need to take care of your body at every stage in your life, but especially when you are still growing.

The food you eat, and how much you eat, is very important to your health. Your body needs certain kinds of food to help you have energy and grow. Some foods, such as milk and cheese, give you strong bones and teeth, for example, and green vegetables are good for your blood and skin. If you do not eat enough of the right kinds of foods, your body may not grow as well as it should. If you eat too much of some foods, you may become overweight, and this can weaken your body and make you more likely to get sick.

**Eating plenty of fresh fruit and vegetables every day is one great way to stay healthy.**

When you get sick, your body can sometimes fight the sickness on its own. If it cannot, you may need a doctor to help you to get better.

Exercise is important, too. It strengthens your bones and keeps your heart working properly. A healthy heart is very important since it pumps blood around your body. Your blood carries oxygen and food to all your cells. Without these things, your cells would soon begin to die.

We are surrounded by invisibly small creatures called germs that can get inside us and make us sick. Keeping your body clean and always washing your hands after going to the bathroom and before eating helps to keep germs away.

# Fighting fit

Doctors can help us to avoid catching some sicknesses. They give us a small injection (or shot) of the germs that cause the sickness. This type of shot is called a vaccination. It makes our bodies learn how to fight that particular sickness, so that if we meet the same germs again they will not make us sick.

# Body words

Words shown in italics, *like this*, are a guide
to how a particular word sounds.

### Cells
Tiny bits of living material from which all
of the parts of your body are built. There
are different types of cell in your body.
Some cells make your blood, and others
make your bones and muscles.

### Egg cell
The female half of what it takes to make
a baby. When an egg cell joins with a
sperm cell inside a woman's body, the two
cells start to grow into a baby.

### Germs
Invisibly small living things that exist all
around us. Germs can be seen only
through a microscope. If they get inside
our bodies, they can make us sick.

### Hatching
When a young creature breaks out of the
egg in which it formed. Birds lay eggs,
but so do many other animals.

### Life cycle
The way an animal is born, lives its life,
reproduces, and dies.

### Mammals
Animals that feed their young with milk
from the mother's body. Mammals all have
some kind of hair or fur on their body, and
most of them give birth to live young
rather than laying eggs. Humans, whales,
bats, and tigers are all mammals.

### Oxygen
One of the Earth's gases. We breathe in
oxygen to have the energy we need
to live and grow.

### Penis *(pee-nus)*
The part of the body that men pee
through. They also use their penis to
put sperm cells into a woman's body.

### Population
The number of people living in a certain
place at a certain time. This could be the
population of a town, a country, or the
whole world.

### Puberty *(pew-bur-tee)*
The time when a boy or girl changes
from a child into an adult and becomes
able to reproduce.

### Reproduction

When living things make more of their own kind. When humans reproduce they make babies.

### Scrotum *(scroh-tim)*

The soft, wrinkly bag that hangs behind the penis. Sperm cells are made inside the scrotum.

### Sperm cell

The male half of what it takes to make a baby. When a sperm cell joins with an egg cell inside a woman's body, the two cells start to grow into a baby.

### Umbilical cord *(um-bih-lih-kul kord)*

A long, twisted tube that connects a growing baby to its mother inside the mother's womb. Food and oxygen pass from the mother to the baby through the umbilical cord.

### Vaccination *(vak-sin-nay-shun)*

An injection (or shot) of a small dose of the germs that cause a particular illness. Having a vaccination helps your body to learn how to fight off the sickness.

### Vagina *(va-jy-na)*

A short tube or passage leading from a woman's womb to an opening between her legs. Babies leave their mother's womb through the vagina when they are born.

### Womb *(woom)*

The part of a woman's body where a baby grows.

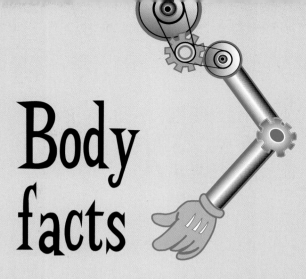

# Body facts

- Most animals are either male or female, but some, such as earthworms, are both at once.

- A human egg is a single cell about half the size of a period. A bird's egg is also a single cell. The largest bird's egg is an ostrich egg, which is about as big as a coconut.

- Men make about 100 million new sperm cells in their bodies every day.

- A baby grows more quickly in the womb than at any other time in its life.

- All babies have blue eyes when they are born, but most change to brown within a day or two.

# Index

**Web Sites**

Due to the changing nature of Internet links, PowerKids Press has developed an online list of Web Sites related to the subject of this book. This site is updated regularly. Please use this link to access this list: www.powerkidslinks.com/body/grow